Hints on
Masonic Etiquette

Also from Westphalia Press

westphaliapress.org

Hints on
Masonic Etiquette

by R. H. Gaynor

WESTPHALIA PRESS
An imprint of Policy Studies Organization

Westphalia Press
An imprint of Policy Studies Organization
1527 New Hampshire Ave., NW
Washington, D.C. 20036
info@ipsonet.org

ISBN-13: 978-1633910232
ISBN-10: 1633910237

Cover design by Taillefer Long at Illuminated Stories:
www.illuminatedstories.com

Daniel Gutierrez-Sandoval, Executive Director
PSO and Westphalia Press

Devin Proctor, Director of Media and Publications
PSO and Westphalia Press

Updated material and comments on this edition
can be found at the Westphalia Press website:
www.westphaliapress.org

HINTS ON
MASONIC ETIQUETTE

Suitable for all Freemasons, but especially written
for beginners and young Masons. A book which
should be presented to every Initiate on joining

By

R. H. GAYNOR

WILLIAM REEVES
Bookseller Limited

83 Charing Cross Road,
:   London, W.C.2   :

CONTENTS.

IDEALS.

MASONIC ETIQUETTE

IDEALS.

The Masonic Craft has grown to such large dimensions since the war of 1914-1918, that it has become increasingly difficult to maintain that high standard of polish in manners and etiquette which has always characterised Masonry and kept it on a plane by itself.

The reason for such a difficulty is, that many Lodges have been so busy initiating new candidates, that they have not been able to spare the time to devote attention to the many little graces which go to make up the forms and decorums of polite society, otherwise termed etiquette. All Masons are justly proud, because Masonry has enjoyed such an exalted position, and has throughout all ages maintained the high standard which has lifted it above all other orders of similar design. Masonry owes much of its success not only on account of its lofty ideals combined with its universal human appeal, but largely to the way in which these ideals have been presented.

At one time, if anything was done at a Masonic gathering, well, it was right, simply because in the first place it was the correct thing to do, being Masonry and all that it entails. Secondly, everything was arranged to fit in dovetail fashion those necessary requirements which produce polish, breeding and good manners. As only gentlemen in the truest sense were admitted into its mysteries, privileges and secrets, the high level was easily maintained in graciousness, courtesy, dignity, refinement and qualities of a pleasing nature.

Owing to the wide opening of the doors leading to Masonry, the post-war tendency to belittle pre-war institutions and praising what at one time appeared vulgar and popular, many Lodges have found that the rigid discipline, the stately dignity and the polished manners are fast disappearing, giving place to the more coarse tendency which follows in the wake of all wars.

Whilst the above indictment may be true, it also must be admitted, that many serious minded young men are being initiated into Freemasonry who will become ornaments of lustre to the Craft in the truest sense of the word, men who are willing to follow very closely the ancient traditions which have made quite ordinary men radiant and lifted them to a pedestal, crowning them with majesty and dignity.

In some Lodges, newly initiated Masons are allowed to flounder about, committing indiscretions, only learning after many rebuffs, what ought to have been taught when they first entered into Masonry. Even if the sponsor for such candidates was neglectful in this duty, the presentation by the Officers in the Lodge should have been so impressive, that the candidate was led to pursue the why and wherefore of each action, realising that every action has some definite significance, otherwise it were mere buffoonery and better left undone.

It is to those who are likely to feel ill at ease—and everyone who has been admitted to the Craft knows the feeling, some perhaps a little more sensitive than others—that these lines are written.

2

A few guiding principles will suffice to anybody of ordinary intelligence who is a fit and proper person to be a Mason. If a man is not so fitted, all the books in the world would not make him worthy of such a privilege.

THE MASONIC FAMILY.

THE MASONIC FAMILY.

Masonry, wherever practised—whether in the cold Arctic regions, the scorching tropics, the sandy parched desert, the wild lonely bush, in the private cabin at sea, or here at home in the most palatial and gorgeous temple—is conducted on the lines of one large happy family, with the elder brother always ready and willing to serve the younger.

Happy family life, with the baby of the family, in this case the Initiate, receiving that pride, attention and majesty which his helplessness, innocence and trust demand. Yet with all this interest, even from the eldest to the youngest, with each one working in harmony for the benefit of the Lodge, without any real jealousies or signs of covetousness, due respect and loyalty to the Master are amongst the principal features of this world-wide Brotherhood. Without any colour bar, irrespective of social position, age, or academic qualifications, these men unite and make themselves one in the submission of self to the service of others.

In Masonry, the fact is always recognised that the Worshipful Master of the Lodge, is also Ruler of the Lodge, a fact which is sufficient to command a willing obedience, a ready response to carry out his wishes, and a graceful subservient manner whilst work is in progress.

These are the characteristics of all Masons throughout the Universe, and to you, my brother Initiate, cherish and support them to the best of your ability, believing that a time will come when you will be elevated to that sublime position; when from your pedestal you, as a humble representative of K.S., will rule, with discretion and wisdom, the men, who are willing to carry on the great traditions of Masonry under your guidance and direction.

THE CANDIDATE.

THE CANDIDATE.

To every man who is admitted into the privileges of Freemasonry, the question arises, how is he going to act during the night of the ceremony of Initiation.

It is an ordeal which a man never forgets, yet one in which he is always able to look back upon with pride and pleasure. No matter how much a man may steel himself before the ceremony takes place, the various phases through which he may safely progress without fear can never be effaced from his memory, neither if he could, would he allow or wish, that any part of the ceremony should be obliterated or forgotten in any way.

It is, therefore, essential that the Candidate should possess a clear mind, be cool, calm and collected in his manner, willing to respond when called upon, not too eager but always ready, show no fear yet be modest, not bumptious yet dignified in his

3

demeanour, and above all, produce a clear, steady voice which can be heard distinctly by everyone present.

To possess all these attributes, it is not advisable for the Candidate to unsettle himself by taking any alcoholic stimulant before entering the Lodge. Nothing gives more pain and, incidentally, creates a bad impression to the members and visitors of a Lodge than to find, that the Candidate, as shown by his unsteady gait, thick speech and dull brain, has, previously to entering the Lodge, tied his tongue, broken his voice, benumbed his faculties, weakened his body with what is erroneously called a nerve steadier, or otherwise a good stiff glass of whisky. (Why this term is used is beyond comprehension.) As a general rule, there is no stiffness about these overrated nerve steadiers, but a very pronounced after-effect limpness. No condemnation of such a course can be too great, because a man requires all his faculties to enable him to overcome the nervousness which naturally exists prior to his going through the stages of Initiation. Whatever may be said in favour of the benefits or ill effects of alcohol, the safest and surest method to give a true impression of yourself is, to leave so-called stimulants alone, at any rate, on the first occasion until the ceremony of Initiation has been completed. Throughout the proceedings be natural and be yourself; shun the worship of Bacchus as you would the plague.

DO NOT TALK ABOUT ANY FEMALE, neither wife, mother, sweetheart nor friend, until you have become more acquainted with the members of the Lodge. Avoid all lewd and vulgar stories; make no comment if you happen to hear something which is not quite nice. Do not talk about your wife wishing to look for the branding marks, or asking what you wear when you ride the goat. Such small talk is out of place and rather shows a flippant mind, besides being antiquated and rather silly.

As a Candidate for Freemasonry, what you are about to enter does not lend itself to vulgar jest; it is to be a definite landmark in your life. As you are to be called upon to take vows for the rest of your life, it behoves each Candidate to be prepared for thoughtful, serious contemplation.

It is an event which should make you a better man, and a more useful citizen, being the temple leading to that fuller life which satisfieth and passeth all understanding. If you enter the portals of the temple with vulgar, obscene profanity on your lips, how can you expect otherwise than to degrade the temple in which you have chosen to worship.

As the temple is the edifice dedicated to the service of God, so your life is now dedicated to the service of your brother. You cannot pass by the ornamental pillars INTO THE INNER TEMPLE, with a mind and thoughts defiled.

THE PRIVATE MEMBER.

THE PRIVATE MEMBER.

The opinion is held by many Masons of long experience, that the Private Members of the Lodge are of more importance than those who have passed through the Chair. This may be correct or otherwise. Certainly the success of any Lodge must depend largely upon the Private Members, and the steady flow of Initiates into the Lodge; because without the honour and the enthusiasm of the Active Members, combined with an eagerness of the new Initiates, the future success of the Lodge cannot be assured, neither can the standard of work be maintained.

Any Lodge which ignores its Private Members in any way, either by passing them over when toasts, responses, lectures, etc., are given, or by frigid isolation, cannot expect to maintain enthusiasm and interest amongst a large number of members who are willing to take active part and even expect to be thus honoured, but who are never recognised or called upon during such workings.

Such a Lodge deserves and rightly gets, that isolation and lack of recognition which is accorded to few, very few Lodges in this country, by a scarcity of Initiates, and a correspondingly small number of Provincial Honours, an isolation which is shown in a marked degree when the Initiates' Roll and the Visitors' List are compared with the more prosperous Lodges. The latter nurse their infants (the Initiates), and stimulate interest amongst their youths (the Private Members), by encouraging them to take active part in the workings of the Lodge, the Lodge of Instruction, and also at the Banqueting Board.

DRESS.

4

DRESS.

The question of dress is one which is likely to raise more controversy than any other subject on which men and women talk.

Most people know the feeling of being the odd one out when others are dressed for the occasion, and you, through ignorance or other cause, feel so uncomfortable that you think all eyes are looking askance at you, making your discomfort more pronounced. On the other hand, everyone has felt at some time or other, that to be well dressed, or as in this case, to be properly dressed, is to feel that glow of pride and admiration in self which comes to the ordinary man so seldom in life (although this feeling of pride seems to swell in a woman's breast more often than it does in a man). Woman, by her dress can become the cynosure of all eyes at any time.

Since the war many of the old traditions of dress have vanished, giving way to a more

free and somewhat irregular style (which if
not orthodox is probably more healthy and
comfortable).

As a general rule, at most of the English
Masonic Lodges, the members are expected to wear evening dress, unless there
is some special reason which would make it
inconvenient to do so. The question at once
arises what is *de rigueur* in the matter of
dress.

In recent years there has been a tendency
to allow extremes of fashion to creep into
Masonic functions, some to the good and
some otherwise. In some cases, the tendency
has been to curtail, whilst in others it has
been to elaborate evening dress to the stage
of flunkeyism. Although it may be suitable
or even a privilege to indulge the capricious
whims of the ladies in encouraging con-
stant change of colours and fashions, man,
as a rule, is very conservative and staid in
dress matters; fop fashions find no place
except with dandies and weaklings. To the
fickle minded and to savages, change and
variety are essential, but the man of iron
knows what suits him and clings to it
tenaciously; he will not discard clothing or
introduce gaudy colours at the dictates of

feeble fashion. Jazz colouring may appeal
to the savages of Africa or South America,
but not to the average Britisher.

· Evening dress for all ceremonial occasions should consist of the following:

Black coat with tails.

Vest: Black, heavy material, or white,
light material.

Trousers: Black. Carefully and nicely
creased. Braided.

It may be not out of place here to state,
that as evening dress will last many years
without showing very much sign of wear,
it is advisable to procure material of the
finest quality, and give your order to a
competent tailor who is known for excellent
workmanship. Although it may be a little
dearer than shoddy material in the beginning, you will find that you will get much
more satisfaction in obtaining a good fitting
and wearing garment.

Socks: Black. Silk or woollen are best.

Shoes: Black patent or glacé kid. Light
weight and well fitting.

Shirt: White, either soft or starched
front.

The starched front offers so much difficulty in fastening, that many people have

been compelled to wear soft-fronted shirts. Some shirt makers at one time introduced a shirt fastening down the back with a one-piece stiff front, but for obvious reasons it was not a success.

Collar: Dress collar with wings, not a double event, but a single fold.

Nothing looks more ludicrous than to see a man in full evening dress and wearing a double-fold collar.

Tie: Black bow. This is very important.

A black tie should be worn on all ceremonial occasions when black vest and tail coat are worn. A white tie is only permissible with fancy vest. Dinner jackets should be tabooed for ceremonial purposes; let others wear them if they wish, but if you would be properly dressed at Lodge, you cannot abbreviate full evening dress.

HOW THE INITIATE SHOULD DRESS.

HOW THE INITIATE SHOULD DRESS.

The sponsors for a man into Masonry ought to give the Initiate-elect some advice as to how he should dress for this very auspicious yet peculiar ceremony. Many men have appeared for the Initiation ceremony in clothes which have been unsuitable, causing a deal of time to be wasted by the members of the Lodge waiting whilst the Stewards have been preparing the Candidate.

This waste of time could easily be avoided if the Candidate was told what to wear. It is not necessary to add any mysticism to this preparatory conversation, neither is it advisable to implant any fear in the Candidate's mind about what he is likely to go through during the ceremony. Suffice it to say, that the average man enters the Lodge with enough trepidations and tremblings without any more unnecessary fears being added.

Give him confidence by all means without disclosing any material information, and tell him frankly what to wear and what not to wear. Do not go into any details why certain things should not be worn, the Candidate will soon learn for himself the importance of such matters. If this advice had been given beforehand a deal of unnecessary nervousness would be abolished.

The Candidate-elect should be told to wear as loose garments as possible, particularly the legs of the trousers and underpants. Many candidates find that the removal and replacing of a very stiff collar leads to much vexation of spirit, and an irritability which is liable to produce more nervousness. The Stewards or Candidate's Sponsor could very easily provide a button hook.

The collar is often the cause of much time being wasted, as also the cuff links, causing very much uneasiness, and it could all be avoided by a warning beforehand.

The shirt front should be sufficiently soft to allow of it being undone easily, and the cuffs should be limp enough to allow elongated cuff links to be taken out quickly.

All metal substances should be disclosed and then discarded before the ceremony of Initiation.

Care should be taken about braces and suspenders, also contents in pockets. This is for the Stewards to attend to. The Candidate need not know anything about this until he is being prepared for admittance, but too much care cannot be exercised by those preparing the Candidate. Embarrassing moments have been experienced by a whole assembly of Masons, witnessing the retirement of a Candidate who has not been properly prepared.

Aprons should be fastened round the waist and outside the coat. You are improperly dressed if the fastener goes under the coat.

Regalia collars (Masonic) should be worn inside the Lodge only, by those entitled to wear them. The whole collar should be visible, and no part hidden under clothing.

At dinner no one except the Master wears any regalia of any description, and he should wear a narrow width ribbon, or other chain of office which can be seen easily, yet does not hit one with its bulkiness.

Sufficient has been said about dress for the guidance of any new member into Masonry to make him feel at ease. If he will be guided by the above principles, he need have no fear that he is trespassing on any dangerous ground by being unorthodox in any way.

Because other members are careless in the matter of dress, is no reason why you, as a new member, or even as a matured Mason, should not pay full attention to detail and be immaculately dressed on all occasions. A slovenly dressed Mason at work degrades the Craft, a slovenly dressed Mason at dinner brings ridicule on himself, and lets his own Lodge down. A man who is slovenly in dress is invariably slovenly in his work, at least, he is liable to give that impression.

This is not written with any intention to scare the likely Candidate to Freemasonry, but as the majority of readers will be accepted Masons, each one will know to what extent reference to these articles of dress is made.

Candidates who are highly strung or of a

nervous temperament should not be scared,
nor made a butt of ridicule by genuine
Masons, because every member of the Craft
realises that the Initiation ceremony is an
ordeal which can be very trying both to the
Candidate and members of the Lodge,
sometimes far more trying to those assem-
bled than to the Candidate himself.

The writer recalls to mind a Candidate
who was so nervous, that being naturally
slow of speech owing to stammering, was
unable to frame his sentences in answer to
the usual questions. To all the assembly it
was positively painful, and each member
was glad of the relief when the ceremony
was over. Such an exhibition reduces the
ritual to a farce, and is neither good for the
Candidate, the members, the visitors, nor
for the Craft in general.

Another case of an Initiate having been
treated too generously, but not too well,
made his speech so thick and broken, that
the listeners were on tenterhooks, wondering
whether a satisfactory conclusion would be
recorded.

ETIQUETTE IN THE LODGE.

ETIQUETTE IN THE LODGE.

On entering the Lodge Room walk towards the left of the Senior W——, make a slight pause, take the s——p f——d and s——e. If by any chance the W.M. is engaged in any way, wait until he is ready before saluting. Do not slap the thighs, neither to call his attention nor from habit; it is the height of rudeness to force your presence on the notice of others or disturb a conversation. It also becomes too theatrical and tends to belittle your personality. If your presence is not felt without such a performance, stand and wait until you are able to catch the eye of the W.M., then with as little ostentation as possible, s——e him, taking great care to do it in the correct manner without any unnecessary flourishes. There is only one correct way to do it; learn the proper method which is the one

6

taught at your initiation and never depart from it.

Remember when visiting that the standard of your own Lodge is judged by the standard of your own expression in word and deed. Your entrance into the Lodge is expressive of your doings in your own Lodge, and peculiarly typical of your own character.

Whatever you may express regarding yourself, never let your own Lodge down by displaying fancy elaborate movements, which more often than not express an empty vulgar mind; a condition which never fails to bring contempt to all sober-minded men whether of the Craft or otherwise.

It is not always advisable to follow in the steps of Past Masters in the matter of saluting; they are often more showy than correct. Even Provincial Brethren have been known to adopt slipshod methods, or succumb to vain slappings instead of carrying out deliberate movements with precision and accuracy. If you are not sure how to salute then ask your Preceptor in the Lodge of Instruction.

It is difficult to lay down any definite ruling with regard to saluting the W.M.

when inside the Lodge, because customs vary so much in different districts, indeed, they vary even in the same building.

When the Initiate is being conducted round the Lodge he is told to salute the W.M. every time he passes in front of him, also when he enters or leaves the Lodge he is told to salute the W.M. If in doubt about saluting the W.M. when crossing the floor or passing in front of him, always watch very carefully what the regular members do and follow their example, especially when you become a visitor to any other Lodge.

Many Masons who are well versed in Masonic ritual ceremonial, state very definitely, that it is only necessary to salute twice, once on entering and once on leaving, unless otherwise ordered to do so by the W.M. or with his consent. It is wisely said: never salute after your first entry unless told to do so, or when leaving, but on no account when you cross the floor.

When you meet a friend in the street you greet him on first recognition also when leaving him, never when half way through a conversation would you think of saluting him. How absurd it would be to say:

"Good morning, good morning, good morning," three or four times to the same person during the one conversation. Yet this is really what takes place when saluting becomes merely mechanical or automatic, when crossing the floor, as it tends to do when much saluting takes place after the necessary admission salute.

This repeated saluting when crossing the floor accounts for much of the slovenly methods in saluting, which may be seen at almost any Lodge either by the members or visitors.

Many of the movements are worse than useless and should be cut out altogether. As stated earlier in this chapter, there is only one way to salute, and that is the correct way, which should be completed with deliberation and precision. All other movements become irritating and offensive to those of a refined temperament. Particular attention should be given to every minute detail of the salute; th—— in correct place, fingers to their fullest capacity. Avoid all forms of slovenliness.

A few words on addressing members of different ranks will not be out of place at this juncture. Whilst inside the Lodge all

Past Masters, including Provincial Ranks are addressed or referred to as Worshipful Brothers, but outside the Lodge all members being on an equal footing, rank is abandoned. One and all are addressed as Brothers with probably one exception, the W.M. always has his title. When in the street, public thoroughfare, or in company with others outside the Craft, never on any consideration (unless *sotto voce*) speak of or address another as Brother so and so. It becomes too much of the "please take notice" stunt, "I am a Mason." In any case, a self-advertising Mason always brings contempt on himself, and immediately becomes repulsive to all true Craftsmen.

These rules of address should be rigidly adhered to, in spite of the fact that many Past Masters would like to be addressed as Worshipful Brother on every occasion. It should be borne in mind, that whilst work is in progress rank must be properly recognised, and every true Mason must be amenable to discipline. Service under the guidance of the W.M. and his Officers begins and ends whilst labour is in progress.

In every walk of life, due respect must be

paid to rank, otherwise all ambition and progress would cease, and this is what Masonry makes part of its creed, respect for all seniority.

The young doctor does not lose any dignity when, as a student, he says "sir" to the surgeon performing an operation; the newly fledged lieutenant does not grovel to his captain because he salutes him smartly whilst on parade.

So in Masonry: title or social rank does not degrade itself in any way when the Craftsman salutes the Worshipful Master, and calls him Worshipful Master and Worshipful Brother because he has passed through the Chair. As soon as labour is finished, they meet on the same level and welcome each other and everyone as Brothers.

It is not the individual that you salute, but the recognition of authority vested: in the case of the soldier, the acknowledgment of his Commissioned Officer representing the King, who, as a symbol, stands for justice, law and order *to all subjects, irrespective of rank and position*, and in the case of the Mason, the acknowledgment of the W.M. as a humble representative of King Solomon.

Rank and title should be given due recognition at the proper time and place, and the only place and time in Masonry is, when the service of ritual is actually in progress. The robing and disrobing in the ante-room is included in the ritual for this purpose.

The golden rule to remember is, when regalia is worn, address all ranks by their proper titles; at other times, ordinary mode of address.

An old army phrase may be applicable here, although in this case it has a much wider meaning than it had during the days of war. "When on the barrack square or on parade, nothing but a soldier with all due respect for all superior officers—when off parade a man."

So with Masons: when in the Lodge courtesy and respect, always addressing each member with the full title, such as: Worshipful Master, Worshipful Brother, due to all Past Masters of any Lodge, Worshipful Brother Treasurer (if a Past Master), Brother Treasurer, Brother Secretary, Brother Junior Warden, Brother Senior Warden, etc.

If you are a visitor to a Lodge and do not know the rank of a particular person, address him as "Brother." The position taken in the Lodge should be some sort of indication as to whether a member is entitled to rank. On entering the Lodge and facing the Worshipful Master, Members of Grand Lodge sit immediately on his right, then Members of Provincial Rank, Treasurer and Master Masons in this order. On the left of the Worshipful Master sit the Past Masters, the Immediate Past Master on the near left, with the others in order of masonic seniority, ranging from the oldest senior master furthest away from the present ruler of the Lodge. Then come Past Masters and Masters of other Lodges, closely followed by members and visitors. The Senior Warden is seated opposite the W.M. and the Junior Warden immediately in between on the right of the S.W. The Junior Deacon sits at, or near to, the right of the Senior Warden, and the Senior Deacon as near to the Master as convenient on his right. Immediately on the right of the W.M. the Director of Ceremonies sits, and he must hold the rank of Past Master, but more often than not, he also holds Provincial Rank.

When visiting members from Grand Lodge or Provincial Lodge enter or leave,

honours are given, as per instructions of the
Director of Ceremonies.

At the close of the Lodge, the Wardens
should vacate their places, by leaving their
chairs from the left hand side, and proceed
towards the W.M. The J.W. waits for the
arrival of the S.W. when they both proceed,
on a level position, to take their places a
little to the left of the W.M.'s chair. The
W.M. does not leave his chair until the two
Wardens have taken their places, and also
the Junior and Senior Deacons, leading the
procession, form an archway with their
symbols of office.

Processional order is usually carried out
in the following manner: the Worshipful
Master under the arch of the Deacons'
wands; Senior and Junior Wardens; Provincial Members of the Lodge; Past
Masters; Treasurer and Secretary; then
members and visitors who have sat on the
left of the W.M. as you enter the Lodge, or
those who have occupied the seats nearest
the Provincial Brethren and Past Masters.
The Director of Ceremonies should not leave
until all other Brethren, except the I.G.,
have passed out. The Deacons lead the
W.M. to the door and allow the members to

pass under the archway, when all immediately disrobe.

Members of Grand Lodge and visiting Provincial Officers usually retire before the Lodge is closed, the signal being given by the Director of Ceremonies for any honours due.

ETIQUETTE OUT OF THE LODGE.

AT DINNER.

ETIQUETTE OUT OF THE LODGE.
AT DINNER.

As a young enthusiastic Mason be particularly careful not to make the mistake of calling the refreshment after labour by the term, "the fourth degree." Nothing irritates the old school more (and by that term there is no disrespect) than to hear a young Mason proposing and replying to a toast and talking about the fourth degree in Masonry.

There is no such thing in Craft Masonry. The dinner or whatever refreshment may be taken is not essential to the principles of Freemasonry, although it certainly adds to its charm. There are many occasions when the spirit of brotherhood has received a decided stimulus over the festive board, but Masonry can exist, as it has done during difficult periods, without the festive board, which really is only an adjunct.

Seafaring brethren and others, who have travelled in foreign climes can always record with pride how a few members of the Craft have met together in a bond of union, completing their labour but without any refreshment, under strange circumstances and weird surroundings, and even with strange companions as their guests. Only men who have come into contact with such strange experiences can fully realise to what extent Freemasonry is universally spread over the whole surface of the world. It is this feature of Masonry which dominates the whole order, not the grand sumptuous dinner, the more modest lunch, or the light refreshment. These are crumbs by the wayside compared with the feast which the fellowship of brotherly love provides, when friend and foe, rich man, poor man, black man, white man, can shake hands and call each other brother.

The great foundations on which this universal stately edifice has been built are rooted in the eternal (or profound) depths of Brotherly Love, Relief and Truth. Is there any other institution in the world which can claim such a powerful and wonderful "bond of union" as this peculiar system of morality which is veiled in symbols and allegory?

In some cases, there is the tendency to look upon the repast as the "be-all and end-all" of Freemasonry, but he is a very impoverished Mason who lives only for the dinner and social festivities. His Masonic life is bare and starved; he has been robbed of that fullness of life which every true Mason enjoys. In his own heart he knows that he is a disappointment to the ideals of Masonry, because he has grasped the shadow and let go his hold on the substance of the Institution.

Masonry is something more than dinners and socials; it is morality for the individual. To be wise, never refer to the refreshment after labour as "the fourth degree," at any rate, do not refer to it as such when called upon to respond to a toast.

To all and sundry, remember that in Lodges where pride is taken in being *au fait* to speak of a fourth degree is asking for trouble, and probably a prompt reminder, that such things are not done in this Lodge, fourth degrees being unknown to its members.

THE INITIATE AT DINNER.

THE INITIATE AT DINNER.

After the ceremony of Initiation, the newly made Mason will receive congratulations from most of the brethren who were fortunate enough to witness the Initiation.

To the Initiate who would be wise, do not rush off and attempt to restore that composure of mind and body, which the ordeal of Initiation has naturally disturbed, by gulping alcoholic liquid down your throat. The ordeal is not quite finished; you will need all your wits and faculties, clearness of head and speech when you are called upon to respond.

Apart from the Master or Ruler of the Lodge, there is no one of more importance either at labour or refreshment than the Initiate. For one grand wonderful night, he is placed on a pedestal, being lionised as the centre of all conversation, attraction and applause. He is also the cynosure of all eyes present, the one outstanding personality amongst many others, who in ordinary life may be brilliant scholars, princes of industry, successful business men, influential merchants, government officials, or ordinary hard-working sons of the soil, or even black-coated workers in shop, office and factory, but all one Brotherhood.

Yet one and all, pay respect and give homage without stint or restraint of any kind to the latest addition, to the member who has joined the ranks as an E—— A—— F—— M——, and "'tis this and 'tis that why so many great men of the nation, an apron put on and make themselves one" as an E—— A—— F—— M——.

Even the members of Grand Lodge fade into insignificance when an Initiate is present. He is the most important personage in the whole assembly. Was not the whole ceremony of Initiation for his special benefit? Without him there could not have been any ceremony. Did not men travel from distant places in order to witness this particular Initiation? Therefore, the honours recorded during labour are carried forward in a more pronounced degree, and with more freedom to the festive board, when, after labour, comes refreshment.

The Initiate, on entering the room set apart for refreshment, will find that a place has been reserved for him which he must accept without demur. In some Lodges (very few—the writer believes) the Candidate sits at the right hand side of the Worshipful Master, but the general rule is, for the Initiate to sit as near to the Master as possible, yet in the midst of all present, surrounded by the other brethren and visitors, and acknowledged as a brother amongst brothers.

Every one goes out of his way to make the newly made Mason comfortable, and to put him at ease. The whole proceedings are dedicated to him. Is it any wonder that this night, above all other nights, is one to be remembered as long as life will last. If the Lodge ceremony during labour, has already made an impression on the newly Initiate's mind, surely this the crowning point of his ambition to be acclaimed a Mason, will create a lasting memorial of pure natural joy, which can never be effaced from his memory.

Success in life may be attained, ambitions may be realised, great deeds may produce hero worshippers, but no experience in

human life can be marked with more pride
and exultation than when a Mason hears his
toast proposed, accepted and received on all
hands with acclimation and sincerity, as an
Initiate into Freemasonry; the most powerful, seclusive and influential organisation in
the world.   It is an order which counts
kings and peasants as one; it levels all men
to one common level, no matter to what
colour or race they belong; it reminds us
that we are all of one stock, that as we arose
from one common level so we all finish on
the same level.   No wonder then, that such
an experience stands out as one of the great
illuminated landmarks of life, towering
above all others, shedding its light throughout all the years that follow, and no wonder
that every accepted Mason in his turn puts
forth his best, in order that those who follow
after, shall have an equally joyous impression such as he had, when he was initiated
into the early mysteries of Freemasonry.

And now a few words to the Initiate. Be
very, very cautious about your actions, and
be on your guard about disclosing anything
you have heard or seen in the working of the
Lodge.   Remember your vows and do not
be hoodwinked into writing any part of the

ceremony, neither by letter nor word. The
writer recalls to mind an incident which
happened before his reply to the toast of the
Initiate. An over-zealous Mason, sitting
next to him at dinner asked if he could
remember the pass word which was given
in secret during the ceremony of Initiation.
On being assured that the word was held,
the over-zealous one produced pencil and
paper, and requested that the word be
written. Suffice it to say, the Initiate was
sufficiently self-possessed not to comply,
although as the desire was to please and
create a good impression, the temptation
was almost too great. It was a very effective lesson to be cautious in all circumstances and under all conditions.

During the course of the evening, the
Initiate will be called upon to respond to
the toast given in his honour. This does
not imply that a brilliant torrent of
eloquence is expected, neither does it imply
that any funny stories should be told.
Choose two or three sentences in which to
acknowledge your pride and thanks; speak
slowly and distinctly without undue shy-
ness or bumptiousness and then sit down.
A few well chosen words in easy flowing

sentences are more acceptable than ten minutes' laboured humming and erring. This is not the time for any elaboration, leave your eloquence and humour for other occasions, they will not be wasted later, they may be on this occasion.

Be sincere, be natural, be clear, be composed, *be brief*, and *be ready to sit down*, are axioms which should be taken to heart by everyone who is called upon to propose or respond to a toast. Especially to the Initiate is this advice given, because after the ceremony of Initiation his thoughts are liable to be scattered, his nerves unsettled, and as he is entering the threshold of further mysteries and greater privileges, he cannot boast of very much knowledge in regard to Masonry. Remember that you have willingly suffered a trying ordeal, and you are willing to proceed further into the mysteries. Begin your Masonic career by being chaste in your conversation, humble in your manner, and temperate in all things.

When the E—— A.'s toast is given with musical honours (and it is always better to give it in this way), the Master and his Wardens should sing the verses as ascribed to them, no matter whether they are good

singers or not. It has been known for
unmusical men, who could not appreciate
any difference in the notes of the scale, to
sing the verse with very great effect, not as
a musical treat, but as a proof of sincerity,
a quality which might easily be omitted by
a much more able musician.

TOASTS.

TOASTS.

BRETHREN, "THE KING," AND THE CRAFT.

The toast which has precedence over all other toasts is that which is given for "The King." This should be given first on every occasion, and no matter what circumstances arise, nothing justifies any departure from this rule. The toast to the ruling monarch is the symbol of loyalty, not exactly to the man himself, even kings and princes flourish and depart, leaving behind all their pomp and power when death, the great leveller of all human flesh appears, calling them home, but to the figure head, and all which it represents in law and order.

The King represents the authority of law and order, without which it would be impossible to make any progress in life. When we drink the toast of the King, we drink to his health, but we also drink deeper, we drink to that which represents the foundation on which all civilisation is built; a well ordered government; a righteous law; a willing discipline; and a happy contented democracy, all of which the King is the representative figure head. At rock bottom this figure head is the symbol of justice, equality and freedom which represents the will of the people, and "the will of the people may be the voice of God." (Vox populi vox Dei.)

When toasting to the King, musical honours should be given whenever possible. The correct way to give such honours is, to have the first three lines sung as a solo, then all join in and repeat the same lines. Unless you are a military or naval member, it is not necessary to stand to attention during the toast, but as many men are prone to slouch, the position of attention is a welcome relief.

Many Lodges have grown careless with regard to these minor details and little observances in ritual, but as there is only one correct way to do these things, and as there is so much difference between the precise way and the careless way, it is surprising that anyone will tolerate slovenly methods, to the sacrifice of that which is pleasing and so very effective.

Unless there is some special reason, such as ill health of any member of the royal family, a grave military or political crisis, or other such cause, it is not customary, neither is it necessary, to elaborate in speech when dealing with this toast. It should be given in a sincere, simple, dignified manner, with little in the nature of loquaciousness, and carried out whole heartedly and full of strength and beauty in song and harmony.

Before any toasts are given, all waiters, waitresses and other attendants should be withdrawn from the assembly, and great care should be taken to see that all doors are shut so that intruders may not hear or see anything of any ritual in connection with Masonry.

Not on any pretext should smoking be allowed until the toast of the King has been completed, and then only after the Master has given his permission. It is bad form to remind or ask the W.M. for permission to smoke. This is his prerogative, leave it to his good sense, believing that he is the most level-headed man present. There is a tendency to introduce a cigarette between

courses at dinner, and although first-class
hotels are guilty of this, the principle is
entirely wrong and out of place.

The introduction of this break in taking
refreshment leads some individuals to take
the liberty of lighting their pipes, which at
once becomes distasteful and obnoxious to
the more refined members of the party.
Why should anybody pollute the atmosphere with thick clouds of nauseous, irritating fumes, during any meal? This very
questionable and pernicious system of taking
food and drink into the body mixed with a
filthy, vitiated smoke atmosphere has
become a habit which is disgusting and
injurious, a procedure which cannot be
condemned in any too strong terms. No
tobacco ash or smoke of any description
should be allowed in any room where food is
taken, not only is it unhealthy to have food
mixed with an atmosphere laden with
nicotine, but nothing is more repugnant to
the sense of smell than stale tobacco fumes,
and to many people the nose is connected
with the stomach.

This is not the objection of a crank. Even
men who are accustomed to heavy smoking
object to this vulgar disregard for the

common decencies, principles of hygiene and sound practical sense.

All food should be cleared entirely before smoking of any kind is introduced. This is only the common elementary principle of hygiene, so much heard of these days.

No matter how much fuss may be created by some unruly members who crave for a smoke, the Worshipful Master should be adamant in this matter. In really nice Lodges the members would never think of attempting to smoke, nor show any uneasiness in the matter by pulling out cigarettes or pipes, until the toast of " The King " has been completed and the Master announces: " Gentlemen, you may smoke."

THE INITIATE'S TOAST.

In Freemasonry there is no more important toast than that to the Initiate. It is important because it provides opportunities in the first place to explain openly to the newly made Brother the meaning of some of the ritual and ceremonial employed in his Initiation. Secondly, it should remind the other members and visitors of their own vows of fidelity and their duty to

10

the Craft. Thirdly, it immediately puts
into practice the principles of Brotherhood,
bringing all to a common level.

For one brief period in a man's life he
becomes the most important individual
amongst important and influential members
of the Craft of Masonry. As the younger
Brother he is feted, cheered and applauded;
he is spoken of as a good fellow, and for
once in his lifetime he feels thrilled by the
applause of his fellow men. "One crowded
hour of glorious life is worth an age without
a name."

Every W.M. is proud of his Initiate, and
when he proposes this toast he will undoubtedly speak of his pride in having the honour
to welcome this new Brother into Masonry.
The Initiate also will be much impressed by
what he has already seen and heard. He
has passed through an ordeal which has
really been a very impressive ceremony,
portraying as it is intended to do, that he
has symbolically been born into Freemasonry. Even at this early stage, has he
not a right to have some guidance as to what
the ceremony means? and so get a keener
desire to increase his knowledge of the
reason for each part of the degree. For

instance, why so many steps in the ritual and why the divestment of clothes?

Too many men become what might be termed "knife and fork" or "dinner" Masons, simply because they do not appreciate nor understand the full meaning of every part of the ritual. Such opportunities for awakening this interest as the Toast offers should not be missed by any Worshipful Master; it is a glorious moment to awaken and explain the spiritual side of Masonry, and should not be neglected either through ignorance, indifference or laziness.

The Master has a choice of many themes which could be introduced in order to enlighten the brethren and visitors as to the why and wherefore of the various degrees in the ritual of Freemasonry, so enabling them to acquire a deeper insight into the meaning of the ceremony of Initiation. Any of the following themes offer ample opportunities and scope for him to introduce, quite casually and carefully, whilst he is proposing the Toast of the Initiate. He should not attempt to cover the whole in one toast, but pick out one theme with which he is fully conversant, and adhere to the one without wandering or losing contact with the subject or listeners.

NOTES.

1. Welcome to the New Member.
2. Reference to the great antiquity of the Order.
3. Who may become Masons.
4. The definite meaning which underlies our ceremonies and symbols.
5. An example of this in the C—— T——.
6. How this is linked with the pen.l s..n.
7. The lessons we derive therefrom.
8. The charity test in the First Degree.
9. The deprivation of M——S.
10. The manner of preparation.
11. The C—— T—— and the point of the N—— P——.
12. The H—— W—— and the Candidate's wish for light.
13. The Steps. (a) The First Regular Step. (b) The Steps leading from one degree to another.
14. Antiquity and significance of the pen.
15. Crafts' Guilds.
16. Is the Masonic Order of ancient or modern origin?
17. Why F—— M——.
18. The reason for entering slip s—d.

19. Admittance into Masonry.
20. The statement of assurance to the Candidate as he enters.
21. In whom do you put your trust?
22. Fear or rashness.
23. Why the Deacons support the Candidate.
24. The Great Light.
25. The Lesser Lights.
26. The Grand Charge.
27. The instruments of this degree.
28. Symbolism and Allegory.

Every phrase, every word and every action in the ritual is carried out for some specific purpose. It is, therefore, advisable to give opportunities to the Brethren to make themselves acquainted with the meaning underlying the whole Masonic Ceremony.

Any Master who allows any of his members to pass through a Lodge without knowing the why and wherefore of every movement, is neglecting his duty to the Craftsmen, the Lodge and the whole Order. If Craftsmen are allowed to flounder about without being instructed in the symbolism and significance of the ritual, they become like a church without an ideal; a preacher without a message; an artist without a soul;

or a substance without character, the clay without the breath of life.

It is the spiritual side of Masonry which is the driving power; it is the force which creates, sustains and develops the Craft; it is the alpha and omega—the whole existence of this world-wide Brotherhood of man. The breath of life in Masonry is as important as it is in all human institutions.

A wise Master will take this duty upon himself to instruct his Craftsmen in the knowledge of the science which is so essential for the sustained interest and continuity of the Craft.

The Initiate's Toast offers a peculiar opportunity for this work, providing of course, that none but M——s are present.

THE VISITORS' TOAST.

Although this toast is not quite so important as the Initiate's Toast, it ranks second in the list of many Lodges. In fact, when it happens that a Lodge is held without any of the degrees being worked, it frequently becomes necessary to make this toast the most important of the evening.

As each and every Lodge have the great

desire to create a good impression amongst
the outer world of Masons, and as the principal way of producing this is through the
visitors who visit the Lodge, it naturally
follows that the proposal of this toast is
usually entrusted to the Brother who can be
trusted to say the right thing and give the
right kind of welcome. The atmosphere has
already been created by the brethren sitting
in the vicinity of visitors.

The Visitors' Toast is a toast which lends
itself to an orator who can handle it with
dignity, tactfulness and humour, one who
will refrain from cheap wit, irritating puns
and vulgar stories. Nothing lowers the tone
of a Lodge so much as lewdness, coarseness
and vulgarity.

Whilst this toast is being submitted and
accepted, all the visitors remain seated,
whilst all others rise when called upon and
drink to the visitors.

When the visitors are called upon to
respond they should be upstanding, whether
or not their names are coupled with the toast.
In some cases, when a large number of
visitors are present the W.M. may give
permission for all, who are not called upon
to reply, to remain seated. This is a matter

entirely for the Master to decide, but it does
not need very much imagination to realise,
that it is much more impressive to see a large
number of visitors rising, at any rate, at the
beginning of the response. Whilst the visitors are standing, especially when a large
number of members and friends are present,
it is an opportune time for all to look round
and distinguish between members of the
particular Lodge and visitors to the Lodge.
It is always interesting to know the strength
of a Lodge other than your own.

The visitors who are singled out as being
specially favoured to respond to the toast,
should do so in a few, well chosen words.
Although many men fight shy of this great
honour, there are others who rise to very
great heights of eloquence on such occasions.
When called upon to respond, leave out such
hackneyed phrases as "the work down
below, or up above was the best I have ever
seen," or, "the fourth degree (there is no
such thing), has been most enjoyable," or,
"the festive board has been the best I have
ever attended, I hope some one will invite me
again." Be original in your remarks, remember you have a glorious opportunity to
distinguish yourself, also remember to be

careful in your remarks; you may equally
extinguish yourself, or lose favour with those
for whom you have most respect.

It is always interesting to hear how other
Lodges are conducted, especially those in
other countries. Men who have travelled in
other parts of the world can always give
first hand information of weird meetings,
strange companions, peculiar temples and
unorthodox ritual, but yet all with one
accord will testify to the real Brotherhood
and universality of the Craft.

If you cannot give a description of Lodges
held under peculiar circumstances, or any
unique experience, then choose a few sentences on a particular part of the ritual, and
elaborate on its meaning and significance.

Whatever you decide, take great care to
rise to the occasion; do not descend to a
common level, and above all, avoid any
coarseness and vulgarity, let such methods be
strictly tabooed. Do not degrade the privilege by telling suggestive stories, or by
making lewd suggestive inferences. Try not
to offend the most sensitive ears; if you do
offend, you are asking for trouble and may
bring the wrath of subsequent speakers on
your head. Any W.M. who is worth his salt

will immediately squash the first sign of any
attempt on the part of speakers to lower the
tone of the Lodge by filth or other obscenity.

THE TOAST TO THE MASTER.

To some men this toast may not seem to
bear much importance when compared with
the previous toasts, and although it may not
call for such flights of eloquence, it is an
important toast inasmuch as it gives an
opportunity to the Officers of the Lodge to
test the feeling of affection and loyalty
devoted to the Master.

For this reason, it is often a good idea to
entrust the proposal of this toast to one of
the Private Members, i.e., a member who
does not hold any office of any kind in the
Lodge. Most members would look upon
such a privilege as a very great honour, and
would do it full justice. If this were
carried out in some Lodges more frequently,
the great gap between the Chair and the
Private Member would not be so much in
evidence.

Of course, when the Lodge year has
drawn to a close and the toast to the Master

is proposed, there is no one more able to do this than the I.P.M.

A. AND S. F. B. TOAST.

The proposer of this toast should remember to include members who are sick, and also those who may be absent through business calls, as well as those who may be travelling in foreign parts.

After the proposer has given the toast and mentioned anyone seriously ill, or laid aside through sickness, the whole assembly stand, and sing the hymn, "Eternal Father, strong to save."

Eternal Father, strong to save,
Whose arm doth bind the restless waves,
Who bidd'st the mighty ocean deep
Its own appointed limits keep :
  O hear us when we cry to thee
  For those in peril on the sea.

O trinity of love and power,
Our brethren shield in danger's hour;
From rock, and tempest, fire, and foe,
Protect them wheresoe'er they go;
  Thus evermore shall rise to Thee
  Glad hymns of praise from land and sea.

  So mote it be.

This hymn should be sung with vigour and full organ to get the best effect, with the last two lines *pianissimo*, except for a swell in the middle of the refrain. The last two lines of the last verse should be sung with gusto and double forte.

LODGE MEMBERS' TOAST.

Many Lodges allow individual members to toast each other. This is usually termed "Challenging." It will be found an excellent diversion from the stereotyped toasts and speeches, and is probably the most effective method of producing good will and fellowship amongst the members of a Lodge and their visitors. There is no need, of course, to allow this form of conviviality to become a riotous "bear garden," but, used with decorum, it can be most helpful to smooth and polish any rough edges, irritability, or loss of temper which might, with a very remote possibility, occur through some misunderstanding.

The rule in "Challenging" (which should never be departed from) is, that any member may call upon and toast any officer, member of the Lodge or visitor, but on no

pretext should the Worshipful Master be
called to respond whilst "Challenging" is
in progress. He should never be called upon
to respond or answer a "Challenge" whilst
in the capacity of presiding over the festive
board. The reason is quite obvious, everyone would feel it a duty to call the W.M., a
proceeding which would tire and irritate all
concerned, whilst many other reasons present
themselves immediately upon reflection.

Any one who breaks this rule may be
ignored completely by the W.M. and other
officials; and at the best of times, with the
most intimate friends, no one is quite so
comfortable after being snubbed or ignored.

When "Challenging," "Toasting" or
"Responding" to a toast, do not raise the
glass and then draw it from side to side,
cross the body, or perform any other fantas-
tic arm exercise. It is simply not done by
discerning Masons as it shows a total lack
of discretion. "Challenge" boldly, without undue noisy vulgarity or rowdiness, and
always remember to stand up, responding
heartily and with alacrity to any, and all
"Challenges" meant for you. Do not
stand too much on ceremony. Be ready at
all times to toast a visitor, even although

you may not know him or his name; he may be a stranger in a strange land, and your interest in him may ripen into a sound friendship. At any rate, you will have the joy of knowing that you have brought happiness to the notice of one individual.

These remarks do not apply to the method of toasting, which finds favour with many distinguished Masons, viz., the raising of the glass and placing the heel of the glass on the top rim of your "toastee's" glass, and then reversing the positions with a touch of both glasses in the centre.

This has a marked significance and definite meaning, apart from Masonry. Symbolically, it represents that both are on an equal footing, neither one nor the other supreme.

Neither above :—Glass on top.

Nor below :—Glass below, touching base.

But equal :—Centre to centre.

If you are a teetotaler, there is not the slightest reason why you should not drink the toasts in water or lemonade. No one will think any less of you for holding to a principle.

WHAT IS FREEMASONRY?

WHAT IS FREEMASONRY?

Many religious ideals enter the Masonic ritual and no doubt help to strengthen a man's religion, but Freemasonry can never act as a substitute for religion.

Neither is Freemasonry a form of cheap insurance, nor an open sesame to better positions in life, it offers no magical introduction to success in business, commerce or industry.

It demands that a man shall daily grow in knowledge, and that he shall be ever ready to acknowledge, that all men originate from one common stock, to whence all men must return. It teaches that in the journey through life, whilst many men become opulent, there are many who through the turn of misfortune's wheel, become poor and indigent, yet even to these is due that love which is born of Brothers whether rich or poor.

Freemasonry then, may be termed

12

Brotherly Spiritual Education, for it not only teaches a man how to live, but it also teaches a man how to die. It teaches him how to act on the square with other men, how to grow in knowledge for his own benefit, and how to place on a level all men for what they are, not for what they are worth.

With all this, ideals are embodied, but, it cannot be called religion, although the Masonic ritual and ceremony is distinctly religious.

Education may be divided into three branches, namely, Spiritual, Academic and Material. The Spiritual education comprises all that which is loftiest, noblest and best in a man's life; the education which originates in the soul; the spirit in which a task is accomplished; the expression of all that is best in man. God is a Spirit, and they who worship Him must worship Him in spirit and in truth, heart and soul combined. Academic education may be termed the knowledge which originates from the eye and the brain. Things seen with the eye are reflected in the brain as living pictures, and in some mysterious manner are stored ready for use on some future occasion. This branch of education may comprise that which is to

fit a man for his vocation in life. A doctor
studies medicine; a painter studies art; an
engineer studies machinery, and a policeman
studies the law of evidence and arrest. All
these may come under the heading of academic education. Material education will
embrace all that which is brought about by
the experiences of daily life, particularly
that which is taught by the use of the hands.
This does not connect in any way the
willingness with which a thing is done, nor
the motive lying behind the gesture, nor the
movement of the spirit, but simply the actual
expression of Craftsmanship by the use of
the hands and arms. As Masons, it is
essential to be good Craftsmen, keen
scholars and lofty idealists, guided by that
spirit which is highest and noblest.

This may be given as one of the reasons
why a man with ulterior motives will never
succeed in Masonry, it may also be a
straight answer to those who so early in
their Masonic career grow tired, become
disgruntled and cut away from its embrace.

Masonry is not a friendly society, as
understood by this term (although, some
people may have fears that it will degen-
erate into such in the course of time) neither

12*

is it a burial society nor insurance combine. True, benevolence plays a large part in Masonry, but the root meaning of the word benevolence is "wishing well," and the average Mason never knows to what extent this "wishing well" is carried out officially. Charity is not "almsgiving," it is LOVE.

SOME DONT'S.

SOME DONT'S.

Don't talk during speeches, toasts, songs, etc.

———

Don't talk or move about during the ceremony.

———

Don't disturb others during the ritual.

———

Don't discuss politics or religion.

———

Don't take refreshment whilst a speaker is speaking.

———

Don't question any suggestion the W.M. may make.

———

Don't smoke until permission has been granted by the W.M.

———

Don't give the impression that you are "dying for a smoke."

Don't despise water or lemonade as a toast drink. You will not be looked upon as "mamby-pamby." Water is at least pure and unadulterated.

———

Don't pour liquid refreshment down your throat as you would pour water down a sink.

———

Don't talk about females. (The only really dangerous topics of conversation are women, politics and religion, and of these three, the most dangerous is undoubtedly women.) Therefore, let it be an unwritten law, as of the Medes and Persians, never to be broken, that no mention is ever made of any female.

———

Don't argue against a majority.

———

Don't be awkward in any discussion which may arise.

———

Don't do anything to disturb the harmony of the Lodge.

———

Don't be disrespectful to elders or officers of the Lodge.

Don't offend others who may be present.

Don't ridicule or skit at a man's religion. Never talk about a man "being an old Jew," it is highly offensive, not only to the person concerned, but to others who may have sympathies with this much despised race—a people who are loyal, law abiding, ideal citizens in whatever country they may choose for their adoption.

Don't hesitate when asked to take any part. Never on any consideration hesitate or falter when asked to propose a toast or respond to one.

Don't go home intoxicated—but go home.

Don't pose.

Don't be affected in manner or speech.

Don't be unapproachable.

Don't wait for visitors to talk to you. Remember he who would have friends must make himself friendly.

Don't make yourself objectionable by letting the whole assembly hear your conversation.

———

Don't talk about Masonry to your wife or lady friend. A wise woman understands.

———

Don't forget the ladies' social evening.

———

Don't wait for others to make you feel "at home."   Make yourself homely, and then help others to do the same.

———

Don't call upon the W.M. to accept a toast, unless told to do so by the Director of Ceremonies.

———

Don't speak or call to the W.M. as any other than Worshipful Master.

———

Don't address the Director of Ceremonies when called upon to propose or respond to a toast, although he may actually call your name.   He is only the mouthpiece for the W.M., the organ of convenience, the representative of the Master or Ruler of the Lodge.

MASONIC BOOKS.

WILLIAM REEVES Bookseller Limited,

83 Charing Cross Road, W.C.2.

————

FREEMASONS' ALL IN ALL. THE MASTER. A Manual of Reference and Instruction on Law, Office and General Procedure. Constitutional, Official, Miscellaneous. By A. HOLMES-DALLIMORE, of the Craft and Royal Arch of England, Scotland and Ireland. Crown 8vo, cloth, 9s. 6d.

MASONIC SIDELINES. Historical, Symbolical, Humorous. By A. HOLMES-DALLIMORE. Crown 8vo, cloth, 6s.

INVESTIGATION INTO THE CAUSE OF THE HOSTILITY OF THE CHURCH OF ROME TO FREEMASONRY. And an Inquiry into Freemasonry as it Was and Is, with Criticism as to how Far the Order fulfils its Functions. 8vo, cloth, 3s. 6d.; paper cover, 1s. 6d.

THE FREEMASON'S INSTRUCTOR. A Masonic Textbook containing the Ceremonies of Initiation, Passing and Raising. Together with the Installation Ceremony and Addresses to all the Officers on being Invested. Compiled by a P.M. Size to fit the waistcoat pocket, 240 pages, printed with red ruled borders round each page, cloth, 5s. 6d.; leather-like binding, 6s. 6d.

TEXTBOOK OF FREEMASONRY. A Complete Handbook of Instruction to all the Workings in the Various Mysteries and Ceremonies of Craft Masonry. Together with the Ceremony of Exaltation in the Supreme Order of the Holy Royal Arch. 275 pages, post 8vo, blue cloth, red edges, 7s. 6d.; also bound in leather, tuck-in flap, pocket-book style, 12s. 6d.

MASONIC LECTURES, ADDRESSES, ETC. By W. BRO. A. HOLMES-DALLIMORE (England, Scotland and Ireland), P.M., L.R., P.Z. 175 pages. Crown 8vo, blue cloth, 6s. 6d.

www.ingramcontent.com/pod-product-compliance
Lightning Source LLC
Chambersburg PA
CBHW032116280326
41933CB00009B/871